2003 ✓

From Gopo & Surena

Merry Christmas 2003

D0041618

"Hats off to Dennis and Barbara for such a practical collection of tools to keep the pressure from squeezing the life out of our marriage. Every couple in America needs to read this book."

—Dr. Gary Smalley
Author, speaker, and founder of the Smalley Relationship Center

"Pressure creates diamonds and volcanoes—and most people prefer diamonds. In Pressure Proof Your Marriage, *Dennis and Barbara Rainey share tested insights which can help you create marital diamonds and avoid relational volcanoes."*

—Gary D. Chapman
Author of *The Five Love Languages*

"For thirty years, I've observed Dennis and Barbara meet the challenges of their own pressure-filled marriage: raising six children, leading a growing ministry, and dealing with serious health issues. Their marriage has flourished and grown stronger in the midst of these circumstances. I know of no better qualified couple to write a book on this topic."

—Steve Douglass
President of Campus Crusade for Christ

PRESSURE PROOF
Your
MARRIAGE

DENNIS & BARBARA
RAINEY
WITH BOB DEMOSS

Multnomah® Publishers *Sisters, Oregon*

PRESSURE PROOF YOUR MARRIAGE
published by Multnomah Publishers, Inc.
© 2003 by Dennis and Barbara Rainey
International Standard Book Number: 1-59052-211-7

Cover design by Chris Gilbert, UDG|DesignWorks
Cover image by Photodisc
Interior design by Katherine Lloyd, The DESK, Bend, Oregon

Unless otherwise indicated, Scripture quotations are from:
The Holy Bible, New International Version (NIV)
© 1973, 1984 by International Bible Society,
used by permission of Zondervan Publishing House

Italics in Scripture quotations are the author's emphasis.

Multnomah is a trademark of Multnomah Publishers, Inc.,
and is registered in the U.S. Patent and Trademark Office.
The colophon is a trademark of Multnomah Publishers, Inc.
Printed in the United States of America

ALL RIGHTS RESERVED

No part of this publication may be reproduced, stored in a
retrieval system, or transmitted, in any form or by any means—
electronic, mechanical, photocopying, recording, or
otherwise—without prior written permission.
For information:

MULTNOMAH PUBLISHERS, INC.
POST OFFICE BOX 1720
SISTERS, OREGON 97759

03 04 05 06 07 08—10 9 8 7 6 5 4 3 2 1 0

We dedicate this book to
Bill and Vonette Bright,
our beloved friends, colleagues, and mentors.

Thank you for teaching us
how to live in the midst of pressure.
Your lives have forever marked ours.
We love and appreciate you.

Table of Contents

Acknowledgments

We are grateful to God for raising up Bob DeMoss, who helped us craft these pages. Bob, thanks for your faith to step out and be a part of a Family Reformation. You indeed are a radical follower of Christ. Thanks for coming alongside us in the midst of your own "pressurized" circumstances. We look forward to many years of working together.

Doug Gabbert and his entire team deserve a standing ovation. Thanks for your vision for this series of books and for your heart to see families transformed.

To those in the president's office at FamilyLife, we can't express enough gratefulness. Clark Hollingsworth, you and Julia are another pair of angels sent by God to help lead this ministry. Janet Logan and Michele English, thanks for the juggling act you do daily and how you serve the Savior (and us) with excellence. To a pair of incredible servants, John and Julie Majors, we say "thank you" for nearly three years of outstanding service.

And finally, we want to express our gratefulness to God for giving us grace and the ability to write these pages. You are indeed an awesome God. Thank You for the privilege of being called Your children and for the honor of serving You for more than thirty-three years.

CHAPTER I

A Rock and a Hard Place

As Barbara can confirm, I love the great outdoors. I enjoy hunting. Fishing. Boating. I've even done a little mountain climbing in my time. But nothing on the scale of what Aron Ralston has accomplished. By the time Aron reached his twenty-seventh birthday, this real-life Spider-Man had scaled *forty-nine* of Colorado's toughest fourteen-thousand-foot, awe-inspiring mountains.

He's half my age and twice the outdoorsman I'll ever be.

Yet on April 25, 2003, Aron found himself in a battle for his life. For the first time in his climbing career, Aron became permanently wedged between a rock and a hard place.

Literally.

It was a Saturday when Aron decided to spend a day alone with his rock-climbing gear negotiating Blue John Canyon in the southeastern corner of Utah. This gorgeous but difficult formation is as remote as it is barren. Aron figured it was the perfect place to brush up on his skills before heading to Mount McKinley, Alaska, the highest peak in North America.

Only he didn't tell a soul where he was going. It proved to be a costly mistake.

At one point during his trek, Aron lowered himself between the walls of a tight formation and placed his right arm into a crevice in the canyon wall. Without warning, a thousand-pound boulder shifted, jamming his arm in place. Using his ropes and anchors, Aron struggled for hours to wiggle free—or to at least nudge the boulder. No matter what he tried, he was unable to dislodge his arm.

Aron's situation grew from bad to desperate as Saturday gave way to Sunday, and then Monday. By Tuesday, his water had run out. His strength was dissipating. Worse, he knew the overhang of the cliff above him would prevent a search and rescue helicopter from ever spotting his location.

He was a dead man. And he knew it.

By Thursday—five days after embarking on what was supposed to be a quiet Saturday afternoon climb—this young mountaineer remained suspended some eighty feet above the canyon floor. With no water, no way to break free, and stuck in a spot undetectable by rescue teams, Aron was fresh out of options.

Or was he?

THE CLIFF-HANGER

It was then that Aron had to make the toughest decision of his life. You see, he was faced with the reality that *saving his life was more important than saving his arm.* Time was not on his side and the clock was ticking. If he was to have any chance of surviving, he knew he had to escape before dehydration set in.

Talk about feeling the pressure.

Brace yourself.

With his left hand, Aron reached for his pocketknife and proceeded to amputate his right arm just below the elbow. Don't ask me how he managed that little bit of surgery. The knife was cheap and dull. I would have passed out just thinking about it. Aron, on the other hand, did what had to be done and then applied a tourniquet to stop the flow of blood.

But that's not all.

Remember, he was perched eighty feet above the ground. Aron summoned the strength to rappel down the sheer wall of rock to safety and then walked six miles before he was spotted by a rescue helicopter. A member of the local sheriff's office involved in the rescue said Aron had a will to live. Indeed. He didn't flinch from making the courageous choice necessary to survive.

I share Aron's story with you because his ordeal raises several interesting questions as we look at the role of pressure in marriage. When the pressure's on in your relationship...when you're pushed to the limits of your resources...when you're tapped out, alone, and ready to strangle the kids...when it seems you're fresh out of options...what happens?

Do you, like Aron, have the will to break free from whatever is holding you back? To do whatever it takes to remain focused, prioritize the needs, and conduct any emergency surgery necessary to survive personally or to protect or save your marriage?

When the pressure's on in your relationship, what happens?

Or do you want to give up? Do you allow your spirit to be crushed? Do you give in to hopelessness and despair?

You and your spouse may never face a situation exactly like Aron's, but one thing is sure: There *will* come a day, if it's not here already, when you will find yourselves between a rock and a hard place. A place where the pressure—whether from without or within your marriage—has you feeling trapped. Where the clock is ticking and there doesn't appear to be any way out.

ON THE ROCKS

When the pressure's on—be it financial, emotional, or relational, whether it stems from career, family, or health concerns—far too many couples surrender to despair. Overwhelmed, they even turn against their spouse.

Why?

They have no contingency plan.

They have no margin.

They have no hope.

Most importantly, they have never learned how to courageously *minimize* pressure before it explodes into a crisis and never acquired the tools to *manage* the pressure when it does come.

I host a daily radio program called *FamilyLife Today*. Several thousand of our listeners write to us each year about a variety of topics. Not long ago, we discussed on the radio this matter of pressure in marriage and soon found our mailbag stuffed with stories from couples who felt the squeeze.

Take, for instance, this excerpt from a letter by a man I'll call Justin (in this book the names of our listeners have been changed). He and his wife were ill-prepared for the pressures that blindsided them and nearly crushed the life out of their marriage.

"My family has gone through a four-year period of extensive trial," Justin writes. "We've had death, severe illness, business failure, spiritual testing, and emotional distress. Recently, because I saw my wife's mental state become horrific, I started hiding the bills we had in a drawer. We could not pay them due to serious financial issues, and I saw no sense in giving her something else to worry about. You see, my wife confessed she wasn't sure life was worth living."

Kelly is another of our listeners. She writes, "If someone were to tell me three years ago that this would be what my life would be like, I would have said, 'Impossible. We have an absolutely wonderful marriage.' At first it was financial pressure. Then, after the baby was born, other stresses developed. Our son had a hole in his heart and developed a chronic ear infection. Our car broke down—and so did our communication. Now our situation seems so hopeless."

Take heart! There is a way to manage the pressure.

If you've believed you're alone in feeling overwhelmed by the pressures of life, it's time to think again. These letters are just the tip of the iceberg. Husbands and wives across the country are screaming for relief from the increasing pressure that is pounding their marriages.

But take heart! Barbara and I are here to say that, no matter what your circumstances, there is hope. We've been there ourselves and discovered there *is* a way to manage the pressure.

In the pages ahead, we'll share six courageous choices we've distilled and implemented in our marriage—choices you, too, can make to minimize pressure and maximize marital vitality. Each is a practical, biblical step to help you weather the storms when they come.

What's more, we've devised a simple test you and your spouse can take to help you assess the *level* of pressure that's building in your marriage. Unlike measuring your blood pressure, your tire pressure, or the pressure in your eyes when getting a new set of contact lenses, we've discovered that there isn't a device that determines the level of pressure in marriage. Our test—and your answers—will help you determine which courageous choice to make first as you act to pressure proof your relationship with your mate.

CLIFFS OF DESPAIR?

If pressure has pushed your marriage to the cliffs of despair, here's what we're asking you to do: Take a few minutes to read a chapter a day over the next ten days. Then take our pressure test and make the same six courageous choices we have. I guarantee your marriage will measurably, even radically, change for the better in just three to four months.

Barbara and I invite you and your spouse—in fact, we *challenge* you—to go for it. We've kept this book short in hopes you'll take time to read it now.

Not next month.

Not next year.

Now.

Isn't it time to pull the plug on pressure? Isn't it time to stop the business-as-usual behavior that keeps adding pressure? Like Aron, you *can* do whatever it takes to get out of that deadly limbo and into a place of healing. We believe it's time to fight for your marriage and family. To take back control. To take your marriage to new heights. And to watch the Lord do amazing things in your home.

I can promise you something else: Statistically speaking, unless you take this matter of pressure seriously you are most likely on the pathway to a major meltdown, if not a divorce. The choice is yours.

Do you think it's too late?

Are you or your spouse consumed by despair?

Are you surrounded by what appears to be an impossible situation with no way out? Have you lost faith that God is still in the business of healing brokenness? Has your heart grown as cold as a stone?

Listen to this promise from Ezekiel 36:25–26. The Lord says, "I will sprinkle clean water on you, and you will be clean; I will cleanse you from all your impurities and from all your idols. I will give you a new heart and put a new spirit in you; I will remove from you your heart of stone and give you a heart of flesh."

One of the best pictures of this spiritual transformation is summed up in a note sent to me by a man who succumbed to the pressure, had an affair, ruined his marriage, and almost gave up.

After falling on his face before God and his wife to confess his sin, he set out on a new path. He writes: "Dennis, I want to be a man of God. A man of character, principle, and integrity who walks what he talks. I want my relationship with God, my wife, and my family to be like bronze. Once copper and zinc come together to form bronze, they cannot be separated again. I need that. I want that. I will do anything to make that happen in my home."

Just like Aron Ralston, who amputated his arm to survive, this man faced an urgent situation. What I am about to recommend to you may *feel* just as dramatic. But if you are going to experience the spiritual transformation that really changes things, that truly affects the pressure you are experiencing, then you will have to decide who is going to control your life.

After more than thirty years of facing pressure in marriage, I've learned there is only One who can *really* help you handle the pressure you are experiencing.

Read on to discover how He wants to help you pressure proof your marriage.

Chapter 2

Between "I Do"
and "See Ya Later"

The relationship gurus have it wrong.

For years, we've been told that poor communication, financial troubles, and sexual incompatibility are the primary reasons marriages end in divorce. Without question, these aspects of married life fuel the isolation that can kill a marriage. But today's psychologists have overlooked a far greater threat to marital success.

Pressure.

Recently I (Dennis) had my annual physical exam. While answering my doctor's questions, it came up that I was writing a book on pressure. With no prompting from me, he said, "I believe pressure is by far the greatest cause of disease." He went on to describe how the body's immune system is sapped of its protective powers by pressure. My doctor's theory was backed up by a recent study which found that older people under chronic stress had higher-than-normal levels of a protein linked to a host of diseases.[1]

In the same way, pressure and stress sap the life out of a marriage and family. Barbara and I are convinced that *pressure is the silent killer of most marriages in this country*. It is the number one undiagnosed destroyer of marriages and families in the twenty-first century.

A couple can have great communication, enjoy dynamic sex, and make plenty of money, but that's not enough. Their marriage is still vulnerable to the relentless, constant force of pressure that threatens to destroy even the best of relationships.

We know.

Even after three-plus decades of marriage, we are still vigilant in our efforts to mitigate and manage the pressures which close in on us from all sides. We've determined that what is needed to manage pressure today is *courage*.

Heroic, hill-charging courage.

When it comes to the relentless pace of life, this culture takes no captives. You are in a battle for the very life of your marriage and family. And battles demand courage. If you boldly follow the lead of the Holy Spirit in this fight and make the six courageous choices you'll discover in this book, you and your spouse will be amazed at how it will revolutionize your marriage.

Of course, to win this battle you'll need your brain as well as a courageous heart. You must *understand* this enemy we call pressure.

KNOW THY ENEMY

There are primarily two kinds of pressure. Some of the pressures you may face, such as living under the weight of a heavy financial burden, overcommitment, or choosing to change jobs, are *self-imposed*. As a culture we've failed to recognize that choices still have consequences. Especially for marriages and families.

Some of the pressures in marriage, on the other hand, stem from circumstances *beyond* your control: loss of a job, illness, an accident, the death of a loved one. No matter what you do, humanly speaking you have no control over some events that come your way. It's *how* you manage the pressure these events produce that determines whether you'll win or lose in your marriage.

Why is understanding pressure and learning how to manage it such a priority for Barbara and me? We're convinced that internal and external pressure on our relationship will, if left unchecked, zap our marriage's vitality. Worse, over time these pressures could *kill* our marriage—unless we take the necessary steps now to pressure proof our union. As Barbara and I have learned, how we manage the multitude of pressures targeting our relationship will ultimately determine the health and longevity of our marriage. These pages are the result of more than thirty-one years of lessons learned on the battlefield of life.

RUNNING ON EMPTY

If you are like most Americans, I bet you're overcommitted, sleep-deprived, frazzled, running on empty, and longing for just FIVE MINUTES alone. An oasis of no phone calls. No interruptions. Nobody pulling at your leg. No noise. No demands. And, if you are like most married Americans, I imagine you fall into one of three groups of people.

The first are couples, typically newlyweds, who are cruising down the highway of life in a convertible with the top down. The sun is shining. A favorite CD is playing love songs. Their fingers are entwined as they hold hands. She rests her head on his shoulder, and he plants an occasional peck on her cheek. This Scripture is taped to the dashboard: "I belong to my lover, and his desire is for me" (Song of Songs 7:10).

The road rolls out before them like a plush red carpet. They don't have a care in the world. Oh, sure, there may be the occasional bug hitting the windshield reminding them that life isn't perfect. But for the most part, their relationship is like a Sunday afternoon drive on a warm spring day. You might call this the "face to face" couple. Like two lovebirds on a perch, they are constantly preening each other.

That's because they haven't reached the bend in the road called "Pressure Point."

A typical couple in the second group, meanwhile, has traded in their convertible for a minivan. With toddlers strapped into government-required seating, smashed Cheerios everywhere, and sippy cups rolling around on a juice-stained carpet, their relationship is showing signs of the strains that parenthood inevitably brings. This is the "side by side" couple. It takes everything they have just to make it through the pressures of the day.

> "Love keeps no record of wrongs."

Indeed, the pressures of raising children, paying the bills, and juggling endless social, job, and church commitments has drawn their focus outward. Make no mistake, this is when pressure, like a thief in the night, sneaks into a marriage with the intent of robbing a couple of their love, joy, and vigor while sabotaging their commitment. As pressure overwhelms them, this couple struggles to remember that "[Love] is not rude, it is not self-seeking, it is not easily angered, it keeps no record of wrongs" (1 Corinthians 13:5).

This couple is negotiating a section of road that is constantly under construction, with detours, delays, and dangers. It's called "Pressure Canyon."

A couple in the third group drives "his" and "hers" cars and is typically headed in opposite directions at all hours of the day and night. Their house is more like a motel than a home. This husband and wife rarely share the same space.

Like ships passing in the night, this couple is living "back to back." Intimacy died long ago. Friction, harsh words, verbal jabs, and anxiety characterize what little interaction they share. They've lost sight of the apostle Paul's encouragement to "Be kind and compassionate to one another, forgiving each other, just as in Christ God forgave you" (Ephesians 4:32).

In some cases, the intimacy they once had has been redirected—dangerously so, I might add—outwardly. Perhaps there's flirtation with a coworker...or dabbling in pornography...or chatting with a "friend" of the opposite sex on the Internet. Far too often, one member of this couple is teetering on the edge of, or has actually engaged in, an affair.

This couple is clearly off-road, without an SUV.

How about you? Barbara and I know that every marriage goes through various stretches of road. But on the whole, which one of these positions best describes your marriage? Are you living face to face? Side by side? Or back to back?

Furthermore, what do you *want* your marriage to look like? My guess is you'd do anything to recapture the romance and maximize the music you once shared.

If you find yourselves spending more time back to back than face to face, I've got good news for you. Your marriage doesn't have to remain stuck in that rut. There is another option.

The Rhythm of Love

Over the years, Barbara and I have ruthlessly sought to stay on top of our schedule. After having six children in less than ten years, we learned that if we don't control our schedule, the schedule will control us.

January through March of this past year was no exception. Speaking engagements, writing responsibilities, raising money for a fast-growing ministry, two adult children in college...well, you get the picture.

Most of our commitments had been chosen carefully and scheduled. Then came those things in life that can't be scheduled—the birth of our third grandson, a visit with a friend who's dying, and the lingering illness and death of my ninety-year-old mother.

Face to face? Side by side? Or back to back? To be honest,

we experienced a little of all three during those three months.

But we've discovered there's another alternative: arm in arm, moving lockstep in the *same direction*. What I want you to picture is a three-legged race. Your right arm is interlocked with your mate's left, your right leg tied securely to your spouse's left. You're running smoothly at the same pace toward the same destination.

It's your *marriage rhythm*—unique to you and your spouse, hammered out on the anvil of years of experience. Most couples never get to experience their marriage rhythm because the stresses of life rob them of their relationship before they discover it.

> *If we don't control our schedule, the schedule will control us.*

If you are going to run the race of life and not become a casualty, then you must learn three critical elements: First, to run *together;* second, to run at the *same pace;* and third, to run in the *same direction*. In this book we'll not only help you hammer out your marriage rhythm, but we'll show you how you to adjust it through the seasons of your married life.

You do NOT have to go through marriage back to back, isolated, and exhausted. Nor is divorce inevitable.

Why?

God is in the business of making all things new.

Jesus said, "All things are possible with God" (Mark 10:27). All means all. Not most all. But *all* all. Even a marriage that has caved under the weight of the pressures of life can be made new.

Joyce, another of our radio listeners, understands this. "Five years ago, my marriage was in a shambles," she writes in a letter. "I was the church secretary so I figured I'd start counseling with my pastor. I soon became involved with him. Convicted, I exposed the affair, stopped seeing him, and was fired from my job. My husband, in turn, left me. I was suicidal and started drinking."

She continues, "I learned my pastor had done this at his last church. I was admitted into a treatment center for a few months. When I arrived home, I found my husband was seeing another woman. My mother-in-law went to the courts and said we were bad parents and had our five children taken away. Could it get any worse?"

I'm happy to report that Joyce and her husband attended a FamilyLife Weekend to Remember conference. Although they "argued all the way there" and, figuring it was hopeless, "double-checked the money back guarantee," this couple experienced the supernatural healing touch of Jesus Christ and left the event with several nuggets of hope. They sought out solid Christian counseling and have mended the fences in their marriage.

I share this story with you because the goal of this book is twofold: 1) To provide hope if you've bought the lie that your marriage is a lost cause and 2) To help you understand how to manage pressure—both self-imposed and external—so that you, walking arm in arm, never darken the doorstep of divorce.

Now, if you're ready, let's pinpoint where you and your spouse are on the pressure chart.

PRESSURE POINTS TO PONDER

- What kind of marriage do you have? Face to face? Side by side? Back to back? Or is it arm in arm? Discuss why you answered the way you did.

- How might internal or external pressures in your marriage contribute to the position you have assumed with each other?

- What's one step you can take to move toward a more consistent, arm in arm position?

CHAPTER 3

The Pressure Test

As a kid, I (Dennis) loved birthday parties. The cake. The candy. The sugar high. The presents. The games—like Pin the Tail on the Donkey.

And then there were the balloons—in every shape and color. The balloons were a blast. We'd sit on them. Hammer each other with them. My friends and I would even rub them against our hair to create static electricity and then stick them to the walls.

Balloons were great fun. Still are.

These days, of course, you can buy those fancy foil helium-filled balloons from just about any grocery store. Have you ever watched them fill up those babies? If the worker puts too much air pressure into a balloon, it bursts every time. Balloons are a thing of beauty...as long as you maintain the right amount of pressure.

In the same way, marriage is a beautiful gift from God. But the pressure principle at work with balloons also applies to marriage. All of us experience some level of pressure. That's life. That's normal. That's expected. The key is to make sure you and I are not so overinflating our calendars, finances, and commitments that we find ourselves at the breaking point.

Make no mistake. Pressure in your marriage, unless

courageously addressed, *always* leads to problems—and perhaps to tragedy.

Take Charles, for instance. A thirty-year-old husband and father described what happened when the pressure exceeded his capacity: "One day I just hit a brick wall, Dennis. I turned my back on everyone and everything I held dear. I felt overwhelmed by life, the demands of my job, family, and finances. Instead of turning to God, I totally freaked out."

He described an affair he had with a coworker—while his wife was home nursing their twelve-week-old daughter and caring for their three-year-old son. If only Charles and his wife had taken the time to identify the level of pressure building in their marriage. I'm convinced that—had they known how close to the edge they were—they could have taken steps to release some of that destructive pressure.

How about you? Is your marriage, like a balloon, sailing along on a gentle breeze? Or is it about to burst?

Let's find out.

TEST YOUR PRESSURE

Place a checkmark in front of the answer in each section that *best* describes your family life *on average*. Keep in mind no family is perfect. No home is the ideal place to live. No marriage is perfect—as Barbara and I can attest.

Even so, if you are going to get a snapshot of how you and your mate are doing—and how pressure might be endangering your marriage—honest answers will help you identify the problems.

Ready?

1. At the end of the month, our finances are:

___ 1) Okay, with a little left over.

___ 2) Tight. It's a challenge every month and I feel pressure to make ends meet.

___ 3) Strained to the breaking point. We'll be in big trouble soon if something doesn't change.

___ 4) Melting down. The pressure to stay afloat is about to sink me.

2. Our children's schedules are:

___1) Light.

___2) Full. But we're staying on top of it as a couple.

___3) Hectic. At times I feel like their schedules are controlling us.

___4) Out of control. Our lives REVOLVE around their schedules. It's been this way far too long and there's no end in sight.

3. How is communication in your marriage?

___ 1) It's not a major problem.

___ 2) We need a little help here and there.

___ 3) We have major communication problems, and it's causing a lot of pressure.

___ 4) What communication? We stopped meaningful communication a long time ago. Why try?

4. How do you handle conflict in your marriage?

___ 1) We pretty much resolve our conflicts as they occur.

___ 2) We allow the "sun to go down" on our anger about half the time.

___ 3) We don't resolve conflict well at all. I'm a peacemaker and my spouse is a prizefighter.

___ 4) We are embittered toward one another.

5. When it comes to our vehicles:

___ 1) Our car is paid for.

___ 2) We owe less than $5,000.

___ 3) Our total monthly car payment(s) is more than $399. I wish we didn't have the pressure of meeting the payment every month.

___ 4) We lease our cars and are going to get socked with hefty extra mileage charges at the end of the lease. I hate the pressure that's putting on us.

6. The health of the members of our family is:

___ 1) Generally fine. Just the usual runny noses, scrapes, and bruises.

___ 2) Mostly good with an occasional sick child or parent.

___ 3) Not so good. Chronic pain or illness afflicts one or more of us.

___ 4) Awful. I've never known a time when we weren't dealing with pressure from some health-related issue.

7. When I'm with my spouse:

___ 1) We use words of affirmation or praise with each other. Sometimes we linger over breakfast or dinner and work hard to connect with one another.

___ 2) My spouse tends to read the paper, watch TV, or engage in some distraction like doing the dishes while I'm trying to express myself.

___ 3) Our conversation is abrupt and devoid of genuine love or care. We're polite, but all business.

___ 4) We lash out at each other more and more. I get steamed over something that has been said at least once a day.

8. When I'm at home with my family:

___ 1) Game playing, laughter, and hugs punctuate the normal ups and downs of life. Our home is a welcoming place.

___ 2) Sometimes I wish my spouse would demonstrate a greater interest in the children and me.

___ 3) Yelling, slamming doors, or cold silence is normal. Our home is becoming more like a motel filled with familiar strangers.

___ 4) Most of the time, I try to be somewhere else.

9. Expectations in our marriage are:

___ 1) Generally met or exceeded. I'm pretty satisfied.

___ 2) Some are met and some are not. I can tell there's a little pressure because of it.

___ 3) There are many unmet expectations, and I'm feeling the pressure that something must change—and soon.

___ 4) I've replaced my expectations with resentment toward my spouse. I feel ripped off in this relationship.

10. When it comes to divorce:

___ 1) We've never used the word with each other. I know it's not an option, nor would I ever agree to one.

___ 2) It's crossed my mind once or twice.

___ 3) The pressures in our marriage bring divorce to mind more and more of late.

___ 4) I can't take the pressure in this relationship. I'd get divorced if it weren't for the kids. My best friend is urging me to walk away from it all.

11. Are aging parents adding stress to your marriage?

___ 1) Our parents are either gone or are doing well on their own. They don't take much of our time.

___ 2) Our parents are increasing in their dependency upon us. We feel responsible for their well-being at least some of the time.

___ 3) We are caring for one or more parents regularly.

___ 4) One or more parents live with us and we are responsible for their care. Frankly, it's weighing heavily upon us.

12. Our house:

___ 1) Isn't perfect, but we like it and can afford it. We have it decorated more or less the way we want.

___ 2) We're kind of stretched to make the payments. It doesn't leave much for extras like curtains, paint, or furnishings.

___ 3) Is too small. I'm stressed out all the time because there's nowhere to put stuff and the kids need their own bedrooms.

___ 4) Is falling apart. We're in constant repair mode. I hate where we live. The neighborhood isn't safe anymore. I wish we could move.

13. My in-laws:

___ 1) Are really nice people. They're helpful and a good influence on our kids. What's more, they don't pressure us to visit or do things with them.

___ 2) Are great *if* we don't spend too much time together. But we are increasingly feeling the tug and pull to be with them more often.

___ 3) Sometimes make me uncomfortable when they put their noses in our business. They pressure me to do things, like raising our children, *their* way.

___ 4) Never leave us alone. It's as if they're monitoring our lives on video cameras, watching our every move. We're stifled; I can't take the pressure from them anymore.

14. Our children:

___ 1) Are a joy to have around. We have lots of laughs together and function well as a helping, encouraging family.

___ 2) Are pretty good kids. They seem to have an upbeat attitude. They're involved in school activities and have good grades.

___ 3) Tend to be withdrawn, and even secretive. I wish I knew how to connect with their world.

___ 4) Are disturbed. They've made it clear they hate us. Sometimes I'm afraid of the hostility I see in their eyes. We're feeling the pressure of what to do about it.

15. As a couple we:

___ 1) Pray often, even daily, and sometimes work on a Bible study together.

___ 2) Pray at meals, holidays, or when a crisis comes.

___ 3) Don't talk about the Lord much outside of church. Even then the conversation quickly turns to safer topics. We almost never pray together.

___ 4) Clash. My spouse is not saved, and sometimes disparages my faith.

16. How is your love life?

___ 1) We enjoy a healthy, romantic relationship with a few adjustments along the way.

___ 2) We have to work at this area, but we're generally meeting one another's needs.

___ 3) This area isn't working. The bedroom has become a
         pressure-filled battleground.

___ 4) We've both lost hope that we'll ever have a normal sex
         life together.

17. Are either of you moody?

___ 1) My spouse and I are both even tempered and easy-
         going.

___ 2) There is an occasional mood swing by one or both of
         us that can result in some uneasy moments.

___ 3) There is a lot of pressure created by different moods
         in our marriage and family life.

___ 4) Mood swings are a way of life and keep things in a
         constant state of disruption.

18. Do you share the same parenting values?

___ 1) We're in synch on most child-raising issues.

___ 2) We occasionally have a sharp disagreement on how to
         discipline our children.

___ 3) We continually struggle with our differing values on
         how to raise the children.

___ 4) Values? We're from different galaxies.

19. The past has:

____ 1) No grip on either of us.

____ 2) Occasionally causes my spouse or me tension.

____ 3) Haunts me and/or my spouse.

____ 4) Paralyzes us with stress and keeps us from moving forward in our marriage.

20. The role of being a spouse is:

____ 1) Not all that difficult. We both had good role models and know what's expected of each other.

____ 2) Creating tension in me. Both of us have a fuzzy and incomplete picture of what it means to be a wife and husband.

____ 3) Upside down. We've flip-flopped our roles and it's causing an enormous amount of pressure in our lives.

____ 4) Causing major problems. One or both of us is clueless about the responsibilities that come with being a husband or wife.

Add your score by totaling the numbers adjacent to each checkmark. For example, if you placed a checkmark next to the third response in a given question, add three points for that answer. If the checkmark was next to a one, add one point to your total.

The lowest possible score is 20, the highest is 80.

Write your total here: _____

Write today's date here: _____

In general terms, and based upon what we've witnessed in the lives of thousands of couples, here's what your score is telling you about the level of pressure in your marriage and home life:

If your score is between 20 and 34, *Give thanks. This is about as good as it gets.*

If your score is between 35 and 49, *Begin tackling the pressure points while there's time.*

If your score is between 50 and 64, *This is your wake-up call. You're close to the edge.*

If your score is between 65 and 80, *Seek professional counseling immediately.*

It might be interesting for you and your spouse to take the pressure test separately—and then compare notes. Why? Remember the letter from Charles? While I want to ask, "What kind of man would turn his back on his young wife and infant daughter?" apparently he didn't see the warning signs that he was about to explode.

Neither did his wife.

Both failed to measure and manage the pressure that had been building in their marriage for several years and reached the point of no return. Tragically, two innocent children will face a lifetime of brokenness because their parents failed to control the pressure.

That's why, like checking the tire pressure on your car, assessing the stress in your lives and marriage by taking this pressure test together is so important. In a moment, we'll begin our journey toward releasing that pent-up stress—while there's still time.

PRESSURE POINTS TO PONDER

- Take the pressure test independent of your spouse and then compare your answers. What surprises you the most about your mate's answers?

- As you review your responses to the test, rank the top three problem areas. What steps might you take *today* to begin reducing the pressure in these areas?

CHAPTER 4

The Asian Banana Tree

The Opryland Hotel in Nashville is an amazing place to visit, billed as the second-largest hotel in the world. It sure feels that way when you try to find your room. They actually gave Barbara and me a map to help us find our way.

The Opryland is so big, it takes twenty full-time gardeners to maintain the breathtaking plant life *inside* the extensive atrium garden areas. The glass atrium ceiling is the size of six football fields. There's even a little boat that, for five bucks, will take you on a cruise through the Delta jungle area.

According to the tour guide, who mumbles little-known details into a microphone during the ten-minute boat ride, their exotic plant collection includes an Asian Banana Tree. Of all things! Right in the heart of Tennessee. This unusual tree, the guide explains, grows only one crop of bananas during its entire life.

That's it.

Just one bunch of bananas.

And then the tree is done. At that point, the team of gardeners cuts it down and plants another.

What I find interesting is that God, in His wisdom, would create a tree designed to serve just one purpose. Unlike apple, pear, peach, or orange trees, each of which provides annual crops of fresh fruit, the Asian Banana Tree has a unique calling. What's more, *it doesn't show any signs of feeling the pressure to conform* to the other fruit trees in the garden.

Here's the connection.

A number of years ago, Barbara and I felt the need to discover God's unique calling for us as a couple and family. We didn't want to forget that God brought us together for *His* purposes. And, to that end, we needed to stop comparing ourselves to other marriages and families. We were determined to live the way God wanted us to live and to make choices according to *His* values.

I (Barbara) remember we had been married about six years at the time. Dennis and I lived in Dallas, where we saw the best of the best. From the mega-churches to the mega-ministries, we watched as Christian leaders touched the nation and world. It was so easy to fall into the trap of comparing ourselves, just starting out in ministry, to these spiritual giants.

We had two children at home and very few of the world's trappings. While Dennis's buddies drove newer cars, Dennis got around town in a little blue Nissan pickup truck with a zillion miles on it. Though he never said anything, I'm sure he felt the pressure to upgrade to something with a little more spunk and a little less sputter.

A few years after moving to Little Rock, most of our friends made the decision to place their children in private school. I know we felt pressured to do the same, but based on our values and convictions, our children went to public school. Of course, finances played a part in that decision, too. Who can afford six kids in private school?

While the pressures of conformity pressed in on all sides, we knew we had to call a time-out and get focused on how God would have us live.

BEARING GOOD FRUIT

During one of our conversations back then, we found ourselves asking some very leading questions: *What kind of family is God calling us to be? What does He uniquely want us to do? Where do we fit in to the Great Commission?* ("Go and make disciples of all nations" Matthew 28:19). *How might God use our marriage to advance His work?*

As we wrestled with these questions, we discovered that we had never really hammered out and clarified our family's values *together*. We had never asked ourselves, Where must we succeed? Where are we unwilling to fail? We needed to look ten, twenty, even fifty years down the road and consider where we wanted to absolutely, positively win. That realization led us to our first courageous choice. It can be yours, too.

Courageous Choice #1
Prayerfully Determine Your Family's
Values Together

Choose to spell out your family values together and use them to guide your future commitments of time, energy, money, and aspirations.

It takes courage to decide and define your values in this out-of-control, you-can-have-it-all, permissive culture. The simple fact is, we can't. We can't have it all, know it all, or do it all. Many of our fondest activities, longed-for purchases, and long-held aspirations must be left in the dust. It always comes down to the cold, hard fact of our human limitations and the knowledge that we—like the banana tree—have been designed to fulfill a specific purpose in God's good plan.

We discovered that understanding and embracing our own set of values, based upon Scripture, takes the pressure off. We don't need to worry about how others are living their lives. We don't have to waste energy looking over our shoulders. We can focus on God's direction for *our* lives.

In Ephesians 2:10, the apostle Paul wrote that "we are God's workmanship, created in Christ Jesus to do good works," that we should walk in them. Knowing His values for our lives liberates us from the pressure-creating curse of comparison.

STEPS TO CLARIFY YOUR FAMILY VALUES

Here's how to clarify your family values. First, set aside a date night to have an uninterrupted chunk of time. With pen and paper in hand, list individually your top five to ten values. The possibilities are endless. Your list might end up with some of the following: love for God; integrity; relationships; hard work;

fidelity; family; debt-free living; giving; health; compassion; recreation; Christian service; career; property ownership; contentment; creative arts; hobbies; missions; mentoring.

Now prioritize your top five values, one through five, one being the most important.

Second, get together with your spouse and compare your lists. Without criticism, listen as your spouse explains *why* he or she selected those particular values. You might gain a fresh insight into why your spouse makes the choices he or she does.

You're shaping the identity of your marriage.

Third, pray together for guidance and begin the process of discussing, combining, and prioritizing your choices into *one* list of five to ten values. Take your time—you're shaping the identity of your marriage and family in light of God's purposes. If possible, rank your top five "shared" values from one to five.

We call these five your family's *core values*.

Now comes the difficult part: *Begin making decisions as a couple in light of your core values.*

Let's say you have a top core value that affirms the importance of family. Suddenly a job opportunity comes along—an offer that would solve all your financial problems, but put you on the road for days on end, separating you from your spouse and kids. Now what? Will your core values give you the perspective and courage to make the wise but difficult choice? Your decision will greatly affect the level of pressure in your marriage and family.

What if your number one core value is your love for God? Scripture tells us that if we love Him, we'll keep His commandments. Practically speaking, you will need to decide *daily* to follow and obey Him if you are to fulfill what you say you value.

Let's say "living a debt-free life" is one of your top five values (a surefire way to reduce pressure in your marriage). It will take courage to apply that value as you walk down the aisle of the department store or drive by the new car lot.

THIS OLD HOUSE

Perhaps the best example of what happens when a couple fails to identify their core values in the area of finances can be found in a letter from Mia. The mother of four teens, she's been married twenty years.

Mia writes, "My husband and I bought a house that I totally hate. We've been in it now for three years and I hate it more every day. It's a thirty-year-old log home that's falling apart. My husband has worked on it day and night all these years trying to fix it up, but that is just adding more stress to our marriage."

> *Invite the Holy Spirit to help you shape your core values.*

Mia's quick to point out the impact this pressure has had on their family life. "Our kids have felt abandoned by their dad, who doesn't spend any time with them because he's always working on the house." She also notes the pressure that bad decision has had on their pocketbook. "We had the money to buy the house, but not the money to fix it up. So, now we have money issues to deal with."

Mia adds this sad, final thought. "I have fully admitted to my husband that I have bitterness in my heart toward him because of what the house has robbed us of. I would like to sell the home but my husband would rather see me walk out the door than sell this house."

Can you see how pinpointing her family values together with her husband could have spared Mia years of pain? How about you? Have you and your spouse taken the courageous step to spell out your values? It's possible you might be thinking, *My spouse would never go for this.*

Maybe. Maybe not.

Don't let that stop you from prayerfully approaching your mate with the idea.

But how, you wonder? If you're unsure where to begin, remember, "if any of you lacks wisdom, he should ask God, who gives generously to all without finding fault, and it will be given to him" (James 1:5). Invite the Holy Spirit to lead you and work in each of your hearts to help you shape your core values. We're convinced that, armed with your core values, you and your family will manage pressure and live more effectively.

Why are we so convinced?

Because we've seen Him doing that very thing in the Rainey home for over thirty years. How do you like them bananas?!

PRESSURE POINTS TO PONDER

- Have you ever clarified your family values together as a couple? How about you as an individual? If so, how might those values change with the addition of children?

- Set aside a date night to determine your family's core values.

- Twenty years from now, what do you hope will be the legacy of your marriage?

CHAPTER 5

The Grand Illusion

I want to let you in on a little secret. Whether you know it or not, your marriage is susceptible to the "American Dream Syndrome." Through an endless parade of messages in this media-driven culture, you and I are sold the notion that we can *have it all*—and what's more, that we *deserve* to have it all.

The unwritten motto of the American Dream Syndrome is this: *The more stuff you have, the better off you are.*

As Barbara and I know, it's easy to be seduced away from our real calling, the Kingdom of God. We are tempted to embrace the American Dream instead: to own the big house, to drive the cool cars, to send the kids to the right schools, to have the right club memberships, to take the extended cruise, to have all of the latest "stuff."

Contentment, like a flawless diamond, is a valuable and scarce commodity. Talk to ten people at random and you will be hard-pressed to find even one or two who are truly content.

After all, advertisers parade a colorful host of gadgets, toys, cars, and home furnishings, as well as every imaginable convenience, before our wide-open eyes on our wide-screen TVs. What's the goal?

To make us discontented with what we have.

To infect us with a *desire to acquire.*

Fueling this desire are the glossy pages of *People, Martha Stewart Living,* and Oprah-styled magazines which feature the must-know "beautiful people" with their must-have beautiful bodies, must-see beautiful homes, and must-own beautiful possessions.

And don't underestimate the role of peer pressure in the spread of the American Dream Syndrome. The lifestyle choices we see made by our families, friends, and neighbors can put us in a neverending race to catch up with the proverbial Joneses.

Contrary to what you might be tricked into believing by the pop culture, you *can't* have it all—whether material possessions, personal activities, or life achievements. God simply did not design us with the capacity to do, or to have, everything. Further, the pressure created by the endless pursuit of stuff, or by engaging in endless activity, brings out the worst in us.

We know. We've been there.

If the walls in our house could talk, they'd have story after story to tell in which Barbara and I wrestled with the temptation to give in to the American Dream Syndrome. Sometimes it was Barbara. More often it was my own drive to do more, buy more, and accumulate more. Years ago, for example, we lived in an older part of town. Many of the people we went to church with enjoyed living in newer subdivisions. Those upscale neighborhoods sure caught our eyes. I can assure you that had we not exercised restraint, we could have easily put the welfare of our family and marriage at risk.

Over the years, we've identified three myths of the

American Dream Syndrome:

Myth #1: Getting stuff will make me happy.

Myth #2: Having lots of stuff is a sign of personal significance.

Myth #3: The guy with the most toys wins.

These three myths are primarily related to the acquisition of material things. The same American Dream Syndrome, however, also pressures us into striving after acceptance, status, and the admiration of peers. None of these pursuits have anything to do with our calling to participate in God's Kingdom.

But for now, let's focus in on the cornerstone of the American Dream Syndrome: the pursuit of possessions. Why? Because the endless, uncontrolled pursuit of stuff is choking the life out of our marriages.

Let's take these myths on one by one.

Myth #1: Getting stuff will make me happy.

I was struck by something actor Brad Pitt said in an interview several years ago: "Whether you want to listen to me or not...I'm the guy who's got everything. I know. But I'm telling you, once you get everything, then you're just left with yourself. I've said it before and I'll say it again. It doesn't help you sleep any better, and you don't wake up any better because of it."

Pitt continued: "Man, I know all these things are supposed to seem important to us—the car, the condo, our versions of success—but if that's the case, why is the general feeling out there reflecting more isolation and desperation and loneliness?"[2]

Acquiring stuff doesn't equal happiness. Nor does it bring inner peace.

The apostle James puts it this way: "What causes fights and quarrels among you? Don't they come from your desires that battle within you? You want something but don't get it. You kill and covet, but you cannot have what you want. You quarrel and fight. You do not have, because you do not ask God. When you ask, you do not receive, because you ask with wrong motives, that you may spend what you get on your pleasures" (James 4:1–3).

Myth #2: Having lots of stuff is a sign of personal significance.

Our culture applauds and rewards men and women who are driven to excel in their chosen career path. We subconsciously regard these upwardly mobile people as having "arrived." We tend to view them as being significant individuals when, in reality, many have trashed their marriages, their children, and their friendships just to juggle the inhuman pressures necessary to "succeed."

Take it from the wealthiest man who ever lived, Solomon. He had it all. The book of Ecclesiastes tells us that he accumulated unimaginable riches—servants, forests, vineyards, and more. According to Scripture, "All King Solomon's goblets were gold, and all the household articles in the Palace of the Forest of Lebanon were pure gold" (1 Kings 10:21). Several verses later we learn that "the king made silver as common in Jerusalem as stones" (v. 27).

Talk about achieving personal significance! Solomon had arrived. Big time.

Yet he concluded, "Meaningless!...Utterly meaningless! Everything is meaningless" (Ecclesiastes 1:2).

The truth is, Jesus spoke not about acquiring but about giving away to those in need, because "It is more blessed to give than to receive" (Acts 20:35). Lasting significance comes when we align ourselves with the heart of God and make His agenda our agenda.

Myth #3: The guy with the most toys wins.

Says who? On the contrary, Jesus warns us, saying, "Do not store up for yourselves treasures on earth, where moth and rust destroy, and where thieves break in and steal" (Matthew 6:19). Why? Because it boils down to a matter of the heart. Do we own our stuff, or does it own us? Invariably, it's the latter. That's why Jesus says, "For where your treasure is, there your heart will be also" (Matthew 6:21).

Even the Material Girl, Madonna, managed to swerve into the truth in her latest self-reinvention: the spiritual seeker. Now married, the mother of two, and in her mid-forties, she's apparently sobered and mellowed. She told *USA TODAY*, "Take it from me, I went down the road of 'be all you can be, realize your dreams,' and I'm telling you that fame and fortune are not what they're cracked up to be."

She added, "Every person on the planet is...trapped into programmed thinking that we're all expected to have a certain amount of material things to be perceived as worthwhile human beings." And, "Sometimes success is a curse that keeps you from paying attention to what's important. Okay, I was living in a dream, but I've woken up."[3]

So, what do you do? How do you and your mate keep from embracing the grand illusion that you should have it all? Here's the second courageous choice Barbara and I have sought to embrace:

Courageous Choice #2
Embrace Contentment

Yes, choose contentment over the desire to acquire.

Contrary to the seductive tune played by the pied pipers of the American Dream Syndrome, *enough is never enough.* Learning the secret of contentment defuses the pressure to constantly acquire or achieve more.

Solomon writes: "There was a man all alone; he had neither son nor brother. There was no end to his toil, yet his eyes were not content with his wealth" (Ecclesiastes 4:8). As Barbara and I learned years ago, we will never reach the point of having enough, because enough is never enough.

Contentment arises from a spirit of gratefulness and thankfulness. It is a courageous choice to thank God for what you have *and* for what you don't have.

If you want to avoid the trap of the American Dream Syndrome, learn to be content with your portion by practicing a life of thankfulness. The apostle Paul writes, "Give thanks in all circumstances, for this is God's will for you in Christ Jesus" (1 Thessalonians 5:18).

Give thanks in *all* circumstances?

Even when you don't know where the next paycheck is coming from? Even in illness? Even when the car breaks down? Even when the real estate or stock market crashes? Remember, Paul isn't writing from an easy chair sipping iced tea with a twist of lemon. He's the same Paul who had been flogged, shipwrecked, and imprisoned.

> *We will never reach the point of having enough, because enough is never enough.*

Paul had even been stoned and left for dead.

The more you acquire, the less satisfied you will be.

But Paul knew that *God could be trusted.* Listen to his amazing words: "I am not saying this because I am in need, for I have learned to be content whatever the circumstances. I know what it is to be in need, and I know what it is to have plenty. I have learned the secret of being content in any and every situation, whether well fed or hungry, whether living in plenty or in want" (Philippians 4:11–12).

Will you trust God as Paul did?

You see, material things will never fill the void in your soul. They will never satisfy the hunger in your heart. In fact, that hunger will grow and grow. The more you acquire, the less satisfied you will be. Why? Because of the God-shaped hole in our hearts. Only Jesus can satisfy that void in our souls.

A couple who fails to see this could spend a *lifetime* chasing the American Dream, only to find it's like a desert mirage—forever just out of reach.

Nurturing a spirit of contentment is an absolutely foundational step toward pressure proofing your marriage. Remember, our real calling is not to the American Dream, but to what God is doing beyond what we can see here on earth. As Scripture says of Abraham, "He was looking forward to the city with foundations, whose architect and builder is God" (Hebrews 11:10).

PRESSURE POINTS TO PONDER

- Rank the top three areas from this list where you feel drawn by the desire to acquire, then compare your results with those of your spouse: housing, car, kitchen appliances, home furnishings, stereo equipment, widescreen TV, fashion/clothing, personal grooming, country club membership, fitness club membership, sports, recreation, lawn/gardening, tools, schooling, church involvement, civic involvement, social activism.

- As a couple, write out a statement of your decision to embrace contentment, rather than the endless pursuit of the American Dream Syndrome and the myth of "having it all."

CHAPTER 6

Islands of Clarity

I f you were to point your car southwest of Cortez, Colorado, drive exactly thirty-eight miles along Highway 160, and then hang a right on Four Corners Monument Road, in about a half mile you'd run into the only spot in America where you can be in four places *at the same time*.

I'm serious. There's even a brass and granite marker on the precise spot where the corners of Arizona, Colorado, New Mexico, and Utah meet.

I've never been there and have no plans on going.

After all, the Four Corners Monument is out in the middle of an empty desert, surrounded by dust, rocks, and boulders. Aside from a selection of Navajo art and trinkets sold in the nearby craft store, there's really nothing to do or see.

But that hasn't stopped upwards of two thousand people a day from visiting Four Corners. Why do the masses make the trek? They come and wade through long lines just for the thrill of having their picture taken standing in four places at once.

Only in the United States—where we, as a society, continually attempt to live our lives in two places at the same time—would that be considered a worthy way to spend a vacation. And yet it's a picture of how so many of us elect to live. We're constantly pulled in several directions. As Barbara and I pointed out in the previous chapter, we've lost sight of the fact that we can't have it all. We can't be in two places at the same time (except in Four Corners).

But that doesn't stop us from trying.

I call this drive to max out our schedules with activities, functions, obligations, and entertainment the "hurried lifestyle." Sadly, this pressure-filled, rush-rush way of life leaves us winded, dazed, and addicted to the next item on the activity list.

The hurried lifestyle means we have:

Little time for serious spiritual reflection.

Little time for anything more than snap judgments.

Little sense of where we've been and where we're going.

Little time for couples to share their dreams with each other.

In fact, our hurried lifestyle crowds out meaningful communication, original thinking, and spiritual insight. What's more, I fear we're actually damaging our children in the process. How? By creating in them an addiction to activity, constant motion, continuous noise, and endless sensory stimulation.

I'm reminded of the teen I saw skiing down the slopes in the Colorado Rockies not long ago. Barbara and I were surrounded by some of the most glorious mountains on earth in Vail. Beauty dripped from the trees like melting snow. It was breathtaking.

Not far from me, a teenage boy flew by with a set of headphones clamped to his head, listening to music. The sight amazed me. Here was a kid who couldn't get away from entertaining himself, even while surrounded by the magnificent Colorado terrain.

Look at it this way.

How will your children develop an appreciation for spiritual reflection, for original thinking, and for problem solving if they never receive instruction to that end nor see it modeled in your home?

FOOD FOR THOUGHT

Did you know that there are cultures which don't have a word for "minute" or for "hour"? They simply have no need or desire to measure time in such short increments. Nor do they attempt to maximize every second of the day; filling their lives to the brink is unthinkable. As Frank White, former governor of Arkansas, once said, "To say that you don't have time is not a statement of fact, but a statement of value."

A world without minutes and hours may seem extreme, so rest assured that I'm not suggesting we all move to Jamaica. But let's not whip past the benefits of what we might call "the contemplative lifestyle."

When we allow ourselves time for *creative solitude*, we begin to rediscover life in all its richness. When we give perspective, understanding, dreaming, praying, and seeking clarity the necessary time and space in our lives, we will find more to savor, like a good cup of tea, steeped to the fullness of its flavor.

> "To say you don't have time is a statement of value."

As I reflect on these two approaches to life, I force myself to ponder: How did Jesus live His life? How was He portrayed in Scripture? Was He frantic? Or steady? Was He checking His watch every few minutes, wishing He could cut time off His commute to the next city, or was he able to stop and tend to the needs around Him? Was He out of breath or at peace? Did He wring His hands from the pressures in His life?

In fact, Jesus experienced more pressure than any of us can fathom. The disciples constantly peppered Him with questions. The Pharisees wanted Him dead. The crowds wanted to force Him into a political kingship. Satan yearned to trap Him. Yes, Jesus understood what life with pressure was all about.

But He also set an example of how you and I can best handle the pressure. Time after time, we find Jesus making time to get alone to pray. To listen. To be strengthened. To gain encouragement. To nourish His soul. And to wait on the leading of His heavenly Father. It is in His example that Barbara and I discovered the third courageous choice.

Courageous Choice #3
Find a Place to Ponder

Choose to make room for "islands of clarity" in your marriage...daily, weekly, and biannually.

What's an island of clarity?

It's any place where you can put aside the rush, the distractions, the "noise" of life long enough to reflect and hear from the Lord. These islands of clarity can be savored alone. They should also be enjoyed together as a couple.

Why does it take courage? Because everything around you—your "to do" list, your "want" list, your children, your work—howls and stomps like a toddler throwing a tantrum, demanding your immediate energy and attention. It takes courage to close your ears. It takes strong resolve to resist.

When Barbara and I carved out time for islands of clarity in our married life, the results were priceless. There's nothing like uninterrupted time to gain perspective in the middle of the family circus.

"But how," you ask, "can we squeeze in daily, weekly, and biannual 'islands'? Doesn't that get expensive?"

Not necessarily. Your islands don't have to involve a posh resort or a condo on Waikiki.

Here are a few suggestions:

Daily Islands of Clarity

These can be as easy as grabbing a lawn chair and watching the sun set with a cup of coffee or tea in your backyard. Leave the pager, cell phone, and Palm Pilot inside. Instead, take a Bible, yellow legal pad, and pen to capture the inspirations that may surface.

This is not a Bible study, per se. However, many times the Lord does choose to speak to us through His Word—and it's a good idea to be ready when He does. If you're a morning person, set the alarm twenty minutes early and watch the sun greet the new day. And keep in mind the role of patience while you're in your island space. Nothing spoils these moments faster than a let's-get-this-over-with attitude.

King David writes, "In the morning, O LORD, you hear my voice; in the morning I lay my requests before you and *wait* in expectation…. *Be still* before the LORD and *wait patiently* for him" (Psalm 5:3; 37:7).

Weekly Islands of Clarity

To this day, Barbara and I have committed to a date night every Sunday evening. You can, too. Again, you don't have to spend a fortune on fancy restaurants. Sitting in a booth at a Waffle House, Denny's, or IHOP can get the job done. Through the years, we have used this time to review the events of the previous week. We've pulled out our calendars and made sure we were synchronized for the coming days and weeks.

We've also taken these opportunities to set the course for our family. Because our decisions impacted the level of pressure in our marriage more than we had at first realized, we worked hard to hammer out decisions that reflected our core values.

Together we thought through any impending major purchases, our children's schooling needs, various discipline issues, and how we were doing in our relationship.

Looking back, we can affirm that having a date night was one of the most important commitments we ever made.

Biannual Islands of Clarity

Admittedly, you might need to save up for these, but the benefits outweigh the costs. Twice a year, we highly recommend getting away for at least an overnight stay—without the kids. A two- or three-day weekend is even better if you can swing it.

This could be as simple as checking into a hotel across town, or a trip to another city. These getaways are especially important when you are faced with certain decisions like house and car purchases, or uprooting the family from a good church, friends, and school in pursuit of a job or career change.

Far too often, marriage resembles a shootout between Siamese twins. We're joined together at the hip, but we fight to control the direction of the marriage. We lose sight of the fact that the Lord has a unique calling on our lives. He had a purpose—a Kingdom agenda—when He brought us together.

An extended island of clarity allows you to regroup, refocus, refuel, reevaluate, and revive your marriage in light of this Kingdom calling. Furthermore, when both spouses share in the decisions that increase and decrease pressure, they take ownership of the direction of their marriage, which can minimize tension.

A final thought: If you're tempted to blow off the courageous choice to practice islands of clarity, I really don't blame you. Creative solitude in this hyperactive culture is a rare bird...about as rare as spotting an albino crow. But, as the old saying goes, "Don't knock it until you try it."

Why am I so big on this step?

It's how Barbara and I survived.

PRESSURE POINTS TO PONDER

- Look over your schedule and determine how much room you have for personal reflection.

- Establish a regular date night and biannual getaway as a couple.

- Discuss why Jesus, the savior of the world, found it necessary to embrace solitude.

CHAPTER 7

Spin Cycle

M arci sent this note to me at the end of what must have been a very bad day. She writes, "My husband and I struggle with in-laws, family issues, debt, job security, car repair bills, questions about the children...our daily life is under so much stress! Some days I'd be happy just to get through the laundry."

I don't pretend to know the details of her situation. However, based upon our experience raising six kids, it appears that what Marci lacks is *margin*. Margin is the "wiggle room" necessary to accommodate immediate needs while allowing for the unexpected demands and interruptions of life.

I find it helpful to view margin this way.

Picture a tabletop.

If you were to build your house and live your life in the center of that table, the odds of falling off of the edge would be negligible.

On the other hand, if you were to build your dream home on or near the edge, it would take very little—a couple of missed paychecks, sudden unemployment, or illness—to push you over the edge. Like Wyle E. Coyote in the Road Runner cartoon, you'd suddenly find yourself trying to stand in midair, flapping your arms above a deep canyon.

That's what lack of margin does to a marriage.

Marci is not alone. Most families lack margin. They seem determined to run their lives full throttle all the time. They live life on the edge with bulging schedules and maxed-out credit cards, only to collapse in exhaustion at the end of the day.

What my weary friends fail to see is that lack of margin increases the pressure on marriage and family life.

Barbara and I learned of our need for margin primarily through over scheduling and overexpecting. We repeatedly experienced the false promise of the hurried lifestyle—the notion that "you can have it all." In fact, we made poor decisions and watched our margin evaporate.

By contrast, our margin expanded when we made the tough, courageous decisions based on our core values that protected our schedule from unneeded commitments.

Ultimately, margin is all about proactively making wise decisions that reflect our family's real values. What kind of lifestyle we'll live...financial decisions...who, or what, we will live for...who we're going to embrace or not embrace as friends.

Learn the power of saying no more often than yes.

These decisions will either increase or decrease margin in our marriage. Often the lack of margin stems from poor decision-making reflected by the unchecked desire to acquire. All of this leads us to the fourth courageous decision that helps us manage pressure in our marriage.

Courageous Choice #4
Aggressively Build Margin into Your Family Life

Choose to say "NO" frequently...so you can say "YES!" where it really counts.

Often the most courageous and powerful word in our vocabulary is the word no. Whether in your finances, in your relationships, or in your activities and commitments, learn the power of saying no more often than yes.

While parents around us were putting their children into three or four activities each, we made the decision to say no to multiple activities. We preserved what precious little margin we had with six children by saying yes to just one activity per child, max. Samuel played tennis and had to shut down that activity if he wanted to play basketball. Rebecca chose, and excelled at, gymnastics.

By the time our youngest, Laura, came along, most of the other kids were out the door. Frankly, we granted her the most latitude. She enjoyed the privilege of participating in cheerleading, softball, and volleyball...and wore us out in the process! Barbara and I were thankful we had stuck to the one activity per child rule with the others.

Obviously, we are less than perfect in the application of this courageous choice. Someone once said, "The way you learn how to make a good decision is to make a bad decision." Both Barbara and I have repeatedly proved that saying true when it comes to our schedule. More than three decades into our marriage and family, scheduling still provides one of the most robust challenges we face together as a couple.

NO MEANS NO

In the early days of our family we scheduled too many activities and had too many objectives. Our underestimating and over scheduling occurred at work and at home, on weeknights *and* weekends. We experienced a need for margin.

I recall making what appeared to be a good decision at the time. I had been invited to a prestigious meeting of leaders in Dallas. Barbara had agreed that it was an honor and a great opportunity.

As I was packing to leave, it became very apparent that Barbara was wiped out physically and emotionally from caring for our six children, who at the time ranged in age from two to twelve. The meeting wasn't one I *had* to attend. As we discussed our options, it became clear I should stay and help Barbara. I could press on, or I could say no in order to create some much-needed margin.

On this occasion, I made the wise choice: I canceled the trip. Frankly, it wasn't a courageous choice, it was just the right thing to do.

In that case, I was able to undo a bad decision with a good decision. It defused the pressure and lightened my wife's load.

Those kinds of decisions can't always be made, but when they can, they speak volumes to our spouses.

In recent years, maintaining margin in our schedule has become even more challenging. The pressure to do more and say "yes" is relentless, and seems to intensify with each season. While working on this book, for instance, Barbara and I had a date night, an evening of planning to go over our calendar. It turned out to be one of the most unpleasant evenings we've ever had.

There were a couple of reasons for our horrible, very bad date night. First, we'd been so busy (not enough margin!) that we hadn't had a date for several weeks, much less talked through our schedule. During that time, I made a number of commitments—without discussing them with Barbara.

Bad move.

The second problem was that Barbara had made some commitments, too. We both have a tendency to over schedule. Building in margin has been a learning experience for us. To top it all off, several unanticipated inter-

> *The pressure to do more and say "yes" is relentless.*

ruptions had piled onto our plates during the previous week.

A year ago I'd known our January through March would be busy. What I didn't count on were those pesky interruptions, the unpredictable nature of life. As C. S. Lewis says, "There's no such thing as an interruption, only the real life that God brings us day by day."

How could I have known, in the months leading up to this

intense period of travel, that our family would undergo one of the biggest personal challenges we've ever faced?

How could I have known that Bill Bright, my beloved friend, mentor, and boss, would call me from his deathbed asking me to come to Orlando to meet with him one last time?

How could I have known that in addition to a full schedule my mom would become gravely ill and die—and that four days later our son Samuel's first child would be born?

As we reviewed our calendars, we *craved* some extra margin. We just had to have a little breathing space. That night, we forced ourselves to make changes. We had to do a better job of protecting ourselves, our marriage, and our family. We decided to do the following:

Discuss what kinds of margin we each needed as a couple and a family during weekdays, weeknights, and weekends.

Agree on a number of days and weekends that we would travel in any given month.

Get back to talking about commitments together *before* we make the commitment.

Revisit the needs of our children now that they are adults, clarifying their expectations of us as parents and grandparents.

Ruthlessly say NO at least once a day to something!

We knew these decisions wouldn't guarantee margin or prevent all mistakes and failures. But they would help us to move into the future *together,* arm in arm, rather than as two people spinning off in different directions.

How about you? How close to the edge are you living? How

much margin have you built into your time management, finances, and relationships? Are you, like Marci, longing for rest in the middle of the storm?

If so, you'll take comfort in the next chapter as we explore the role of Sabbath rest in restoring your soul.

PRESSURE POINTS TO PONDER

- Think back to your answer on the pressure test regarding finances. If you find it difficult to make ends meet each month, how might you create more margin in the area of finances?

- Talk about the principle sources of pressure for you as a couple and a family right now. Make a list, discuss, and evaluate.

- Look over your calendar for the next three months. What activities might you cut out in order to build in more time for rest, reflection, and recreation?

CHAPTER 8

Rest Assured

Up to this point, Dennis and I have discussed four courageous choices that will help you pressure proof your
marriage. These are all concepts that have been tested, tried,
and proven effective by hundreds of couples and families across
our nation.

Yet they are of no value at all apart from the power of God.

Jesus put it more bluntly: "Apart from me *you can do nothing*" (John 15:5). He goes on to declare our profound need as
disciples to *abide* or *remain* in Him. Why?

In simple terms, there is no possible way you or I can be
successful in our attempts to pressure proof our marriages apart
from this intimate, ongoing relationship with Jesus Christ.

Period.

Jesus wants us to draw our very life from Him—that's what
the word "abide" means. Just as a grapevine provides life for
branches that bear fruit, so we too are to bear fruit by abiding
in Him moment by moment, seeking the control and empower-
ment of the Holy Spirit.

Jesus knows we need power to live and make courageous
choices. He sent the Holy Spirit to inhabit the lives of true
believers for the purpose of empowering us, guiding us, and
teaching us how to live for God.

And so we return to the central question raised in an earlier chapter: *Who* or *what* is in control of your marriage? Where does your power for living lie? Are you relying on your performance? Your talents? Your lineage? If so—and I state this as lovingly as I know how—you and your marriage are headed for big trouble.

If, on the other hand, you answered as Joshua did, "as for me and my household, we will serve the LORD" (Joshua 24:15), you've taken the only pathway to lasting success in your marriage.

Dennis and I found that one of the best ways to abide in Christ is to set aside a day of Sabbath rest. It also happens to be one of the Ten Commandments: "Six days you shall labor and do all your work, but the seventh day is a Sabbath to the LORD your God. On it you shall not do any work, neither you, nor your son or daughter" (Exodus 20:9–10).

Why is resting on the Sabbath so important to Dennis and me? Because when we yield control of our lives to the Father, when we take a day to turn from our activity in order to abide more fully in Him, we receive strength for daily living throughout the coming week.

You might say a Sabbath rest is like a weekly tune-up for your soul. That's why this courageous choice is so critical.

Courageous Choice #5
Observe a Sabbath Rest

Set aside one day in seven to rest from your work, to re-engage your focus on the Lord, and to abide more fully in Him.

I (Dennis) recall that when our children reached their teenage years and started to look for part-time work, we had a rule that they would not work on Sunday. In order to honor our wishes for a Sabbath rest, several had to turn down lucrative employment opportunities. As it turns out, five of our six kids ended up working for Chick-Fil-A, a nationwide fast food company that is closed on Sundays.

Don't get me wrong. I'm not promoting legalism.

I'm not necessarily suggesting that your Sabbath be on Sunday, although we think that's the best day. Pick your day.

> *A Sabbath rest is like a weekly tune-up for your soul.*

The key is to set aside one in seven where you say no to the errands and the to-do list. Where you step off the treadmill, catch your breath, and regain some margin. A day where you relax, pray, read Scripture, go fishing, take a walk, or take a nap.

An additional benefit of the weekly Sabbath is to remember that *work is not life*. Work is not the central purpose of our existence on earth. *God* is the center of life. He's why we exist. He's whom we serve. From Him flow all good things...a spouse...the family...and the blessings of daily bread.

Early in our marriage, it was Barbara who took the lead in protecting our Sabbath rest as a family. Instinctively, she knew how difficult it was to hear the voice of the Savior over the siren calls of the culture. She was particularly struck by several strong admonitions in Scripture:

"Be still, and know that I am God." (Psalm 46:10)

"Be silent before the Sovereign LORD." (Zephaniah 1:7).

"There is a time for everything...a time to be silent and a time to speak" (Ecclesiastes 3:1, 7).

If you get nothing else from this chapter, we want you to catch this: It is both possible and necessary to create breathing space in your family's life. The Sabbath is God's invitation to draw near to Him, to rest in Him, and to linger by His still waters. That's how He helps us "detoxify" from the pressures of the week.

That's how He restores our soul.

PRESSURE POINTS TO PONDER

- Read John chapter 15. How many times does Jesus urge His followers to "remain" or "abide" in Him? Why do you think He felt it necessary to repeat this so often?

- Think back to last week and mentally review your schedule. How much time was available to actively "abide" in the Lord in a focused, intentional way?

- How might you structure Sundays to go deeper in your fellowship with the Lover of your soul? What ideas do you have to help your children do the same?

CHAPTER 9

A Day in Job's Sandals

Every marriage and family will have its "valleys." The pressure experienced during these dark days can be enormous. Early in our marriage we trudged through an ominous gorge that threatened the very life of our family.

We had just moved for the fifth time in six years, and the realtor who sold us the house deceived us, resulting in the loss of several thousand dollars. Only three weeks after we moved in, I (Dennis) received a phone call from my brother with the chilling news that my dad had died suddenly of a heart attack.

In the month that followed, we were tapped out trying to help my mom recover from the shock of Dad's death. In the midst of that time, we ran into financial problems of our own, receiving a short paycheck. Over the following ninety days, I had massive dental work done and we rushed our one-year-old son Benjamin to the hospital for emergency surgery.

Pressure. Stress. Heaviness.

We were reeling emotionally and financially. But that was only the halfway point in our walk down the jagged trail of our valley.

My brother, who managed the family propane business, was hospitalized with an apparent heart attack. I had to go back and run the business in his absence. That would have been challenging enough had it not been the worst winter in Midwest history.

LIKE FATHER, LIKE SON

In the midst of the unrelenting stress of attempting to provide fuel for several thousand homes, I laid down one evening in the bed my father had died in only months before, and my heart took off like a racehorse. I was rushed to the emergency room of the same hospital my brother was in and found out it was not a heart attack, but *stress*.

Some weeks later, I (Barbara) was doing my exercises at home. For some reason Dennis had delayed going to the office. It was a good thing he hadn't left, because at about 9 A.M. I nearly fainted. My heart was racing even more than his. Dennis placed his hand on my neck—my heart was beating so fast that he couldn't count the beats. We hurried to the hospital, where my heart rate was recorded at more than three hundred beats a minute. And the doctors couldn't slow my heart.

About noon my lungs began to fill with fluid, and at 2 P.M. I labored to breathe because of asthma. I was in a life-threatening situation. Later we found out I had a rare disorder called Wolfe-Parkinson-White Syndrome, and that my heart could do this again at any time.

For the next few months I had extra heartbeats.

Then we found out I was pregnant with our son Samuel!

At this point in our walk through the valley, we had experienced surprises, loads of pain, and a feeling that we were not in control. There was no romance. Little fun. We were at that point where many couples choose the road of total isolation. But a single word stopped us: *commitment.* Commitment to God, combined with trust that He knows what He's doing in our lives. And commitment to one another.

Which leads us to our final courageous choice.

Courageous Choice #6
Fulfill Your Marriage Vows

Choose to remain committed to one another regardless of how much pressure, pain, and stress come your way.

The fact that we will not quit, that we will be there for one another—even when the unexpected happens—actually helps to mitigate the pressure between us. Besides, why are we so surprised when trouble comes our way? Jesus actually *promised* we would experience problems.

Did you catch that?

Jesus said, "In this world *you will have trouble.*" Then, in the next breath, He quickly pointed out, "But take heart! I have overcome the world" (John 16:33). Expect the unexpected. Suffering. Trials. Difficulties. But don't give up. Jesus will be there in the midst of your troubles.

Modern society is still suffering from the sickness of the

"Me Generation," which has contaminated the covenant of marriage. The selfish, Me-Gen person says in effect, *When marriage serves my purpose, I'm on board. When it ceases to make me happy, when it's too much effort, when the unexpected shows up and creates additional pressure, I'm out of here.* Some leave physically and move out...others leave emotionally and withdraw.

Sadly, they've lost sight of their vows: "for better *and* for worse."

Let us suggest three ways your commitment to honoring your vows can sustain you in the valley and reduce the pressure on your marriage at the same time.

WHEN THREE BECOME ONE

First, understand that your marriage commitment is a covenant between three, not two. On our wedding day, I (Dennis) entered into a covenant with both Barbara and God. Our marriage is not a contract, but a sacred cord of three strands that will not be easily broken (see Ecclesiastes 4:12).

Your covenant with God and one another is the strength of your relationship and the key to managing the pressure of the valley together. If your vows are weak, your ability to make courageous choices together is diminished.

Second, your vows mean that you will forgive one another. Again, Scripture says: "Be kind and compassionate to one another, forgiving each other, just as in Christ God forgave you" (Ephesians 4:32).

No marriage is a perpetual walk through the daisies. There

will be unmet expectations, unwise decisions, troubles with schedules and finances, and unexpected pressures that will rattle your home like a storm. When hurt and disappointment come, however, our vows demand that we forgive one another. Forgiveness is not optional in managing pressure in marriage.

It is life and breath.

Finally, your vows mean your commitment is enduring. When the pressure becomes relentless, white-hot, and intense…when the cultural voices around you entice you to "look out for yourself" and quit your marriage, your vows shout: DON'T!

Or, as several of my kids say, "Deal with it."

Quitting may reduce pressure temporarily, but I promise you a broken marriage and family will only add truckloads of pressure over a lifetime. It takes courage to lean on God and the promises of His Word and keep our vows "'til death do us part."

> *Forgiveness is not optional in managing pressure in marriage. It is life and breath.*

I received a letter from a lady named Alisa not long ago. Her courageous commitment shines through every word: "I'm a forty-eight-year-old mother of five children, including a set of three-and-a-half-year-old boy/girl twins. I now care for my aging mother-in-law (who lives with us) and I also care for my three little granddaughters during the day."

I'm worn out just reading her letter.

She continues, "Am I stressed? Yes. Can I do this day in and out? Actually, yes. Where do I get my strength? I have none of my own. Truly it is the Holy Spirit living in me that makes all things possible."

When Alisa got married, I'm sure she never expected to be carrying that kind of load. Does she walk away? No. Instead, she remains faithful to her commitment, trusts the Lord to be her strength, and remains a living testimony of what God can do when we remain committed—even in "impossible" circumstances.

PRESSURE POINTS TO PONDER

- Can you think of a time when you and your spouse walked a mile in Job's sandals? What sustained you during that difficult time? Discuss what you will do differently the next time you're in the valley.

- If your marriage were pushed to the edge today by an unforeseen pressure point, how strong is your commitment to hang in there? Why not bow in prayer together and reaffirm your marriage covenant with God and one another?

CHAPTER 10

Coming Attractions

I (Dennis) have always been a curious person, so when a speaking opportunity took me to the state of Washington a year after the volcanic eruption of Mount St. Helens, I jumped at the chance to see the devastation there.

A friend and I drove to the end of the road leading up to this magnificent landmark. But because we were in a canyon some fifteen miles away, the only thing we could see was a milky gray stream carrying ash from the volcano. Just then, at the end of the road, we spotted a helicopter. It must have been a *very* slow day because the pilot made us a deal we couldn't refuse: Our very own bird's-eye view of the crater.

Once airborne, we saw what was left of the mountain. It reached into the blue sky—its fury spent, but still sullen and dangerous. As we flew toward it I was struck by the fact there was nothing growing. Nothing green could be seen for miles.

The three-hundred-foot-thick wave of super-heated ash and melted snow had swept down the mountain at thirty miles per hour, blanketing everything in its path. Every living thing. The destruction was so complete that it looked like an atomic bomb had exploded. Massive tree trunks lay like toothpicks, all facing the same direction after bowing to the thunderous explosion that blew a third of the mountain away.

Our flight circled the mountain. As we hovered in front of the smoldering cone, the pilot assured us that the volcano would not erupt anytime soon. The thought crossed my mind that neither of us had called home to tell our wives what we were doing. If the old lady below us decided to blow her top again, we would have been vaporized!

Interestingly, Mount St. Helens had been dormant for more than a hundred years. Who would have guessed that beneath the surface catastrophic pressures were building? Imagine the surprise when the seismologists' warnings of an impending eruption began to roll in.

FIRE AND RAIN

A full month of warnings, data, and authoritative scientific proclamations filled the news. Some, however, like mountain man Harry Truman, chose to ignore the seismological alarms. Harry was a stubborn old codger who lived at the end of Spirit Lake. I recall watching Harry as he told the news media that all the learned authorities didn't know what they were talking about.

I could see why Harry didn't want to pack his bags. His house was nestled in lush forests of towering pines dotted with clumps of bright wildflowers. Spirit Lake was pristine, like a diamond reflecting the pure blue sky. It was his home, and the old man simply didn't want to leave.

And he didn't. He ignored the warnings, and his decision cost him. On May 18, 1980, in a matter of seconds, the volcano leveled Spirit Lake...the pristine forest...the majestic pines...and Harry.

There's a lesson in his story for us. Toward the beginning of this little book, Barbara and I said we believe pressure is the leading cause of divorce today. Far too many couples are living life like Harry.

Ignoring the warning signs that the pressure was reaching explosive levels, Harry sought no wise counsel. He ignored the pleas of those who loved him. *But ignoring the mounting pressure didn't change the reality.* And in the end he was a casualty of pressure.

Unlike others who sized up the situation and took immediate action to survive, Harry disregarded the danger signals.

EXPLOSIVE IMPLICATIONS

How about you?

Are you tempted to ignore the warning signs that your relationship may be under too much pressure, or worse, about to blow up? How much margin have you built into your family's schedule? How close to the edge are you playing it with your finances?

What about the kids...are they becoming adrenaline junkies? Or do you help them see the value in Sabbath rest and reflection? Do you and your spouse make time to regularly visit islands of clarity in order to gain needed perspective? Have you taken the time to clarify your core values together in order to minimize the pressure which comes as a result of poor planning and poor choices?

Believe me, Barbara and I still do not manage pressure perfectly. But if there's one thing we've learned over the years, it's that there are basically two ways to handle our marriage: With God at the center or with ourselves at the center. Look at the differences and then guess which approach minimizes pressure:

With God at the center there's...
    Rest
    Planning time
    Margin
    Core values
    Purposeful living

With ourselves at the center there's...
    Endless activity and weariness
    No time to ponder
    Overloaded schedules
    Inconsistent, feelings-based values
    An empty life

I'm thankful that my wife loves me enough to walk arm in arm as we seek to live a God-centered marriage. And when we make mistakes, when we let the pressure build between us, I know she is committed to taking the steps necessary to get our relationship back on track.

After all, marriage is not a hundred-yard dash. It's a marathon.

Far too many toss in the towel when the pressure's on rather than turn to the Lord who promises His grace is sufficient and His power is made evident in weakness.

As I worked on this book, it struck me that these decisions, these six courageous choices, are like making deposits into the bank of a pressure proofed marriage. How?

Each time we apply our core values to our decisions…

each time we embrace contentment…

each time we visit the islands of clarity…

each time we create margin…

each time we use the Sabbath as it was intended…

and each time we make provision for the unexpected, we're saying *no* to pressure, and *yes* to winning in our marriage.

How about you? Will you rise to the challenge to pressure proof your marriage? We pray that you will indeed embrace these six courageous choices. For the sake of your marriage. For the benefit of your family. And for the glory of God.

The publisher and author would love to hear your comments about this book. *Please contact us at:* www.multnomah.net/rainey

Notes

1. Jacqueline Stenson, "Extra Stress Stresses Immune System, Too," *Reuters Health,* 30 June 2003.

2. Chris Heath, "The Unbearable Bradness of Being," *Rolling Stone,* 28 October 1999.

3. "The Material Girl concludes after 20 years that, yes, it's all an illusion," *USA Today,* 18 April 2003, 11D.

Hear Dennis Rainey discuss these and other vital topics on radio. For a list of stations nearest you, as well as for a wealth of marriage and family resources, visit our wesite at www.FamilyLife.com or contact us at 1-800-FLTODAY.

BIG CHANGE

PRESSURE PROOF YOUR MARRIAGE
Family First Series, #3
DENNIS & BARBARA RAINEY ISBN 1-59052-211-7

Dennis and Barbara Rainey show you how to use pressure to your benefit, building intimacy with each other and with the Lord.

TWO HEARTS PRAYING AS ONE
Family First Series, #2
DENNIS & BARBARA RAINEY ISBN 1-59052-035-1

Praying together daily is the best thing you can do for your marriage. Start right away with Dennis and Barbara Rainey's interactive guide!

GROWING A SPIRITUALLY STRONG FAMILY
Family First Series, #1
DENNIS & BARBARA RAINEY ISBN 1-57673-778-0

Down-to-earth advice, encouraging stories, timely insights, and life-changing truths from FamilyLife's Dennis and Barbara Rainey direct parents on the path to leaving a godly family legacy.

WRESTLING WITH GOD
Prayer That Never Gives Up
GREG LAURIE ISBN 1-59052-044-0

You struggle with God in your own unique way. See how your struggle can result in the most rewarding relationship with Him!

SMALL BOOKS
BIG CHANGE™

BIG CHANGE

THE PURITY PRINCIPLE
God's Safeguards for Life's Dangerous Trails
RANDY ALCORN ISBN 1-59052-195-1

God has placed warning signs and guardrails to keep us from
plunging off the cliff. Find straight talk about sexual purity in
Randy Alcorn's one-stop handbook for you, your family, and
your church.

THE GRACE AND TRUTH PARADOX
Responding with Christlike Balance
RANDY ALCORN ISBN 1-59052-065-3

Living like Christ is a lot to ask! Discover Randy Alcorn's
two-point checklist for Christlikeness—and begin to measure
everything by the simple test of grace and truth.

THE TREASURE PRINCIPLE
Discovering the Secret of Joyful Giving
RANDY ALCORN ISBN 1-57673-780-2

Bestselling author Randy Alcorn uncovers a revolutionary
key to spiritual transformation: joyful giving!
THE TREASURE PRINCIPLE BIBLE STUDY
ISBN 1-59052-187-0

WHAT THE SPIRIT IS SAYING TO THE CHURCHES
HENRY BLACKABY ISBN 1-59052-036-X

Learn how to listen to what the Holy Spirit is saying to you
and to your church. Don't miss this release from Henry Blackaby,
bestselling author of *Experiencing God*.
WHAT THE SPIRIT IS SAYING TO THE CHURCHES BIBLE STUDY
ISBN 1-59052-216-8

SMALL BOOKS
BIG CHANGE

How Good Is Good Enough?
Andy Stanley ISBN 1-59052-274-5
(Available October 2003)

Find out why Jesus taught that goodness is not even a requirement to enter heaven—and why Christianity is beyond fair.

A Little Pot of Oil
Jill Briscoe ISBN 1-59052-234-6
(Available October 2003)

What if He's asking you to pour out more than you can give? Step into the forward motion of God's love—and find the power of the Holy Spirit!

In the Secret Place
For God and You Alone
J. Otis Ledbetter ISBN 1-59052-252-4
(Available September 2003)

Receive answers to some of life's most perplexing questions—and find deeper fellowship alone in the place where God dwells.

The Air I Breathe
Worship as a Way of Life
Louie Giglio ISBN 1-59052-153-6

When we are awakened to the wonder of God's character and the cross of Christ, all of life becomes worship unto God.

SMALL BOOKS
BIG CHANGE

BIG CHANGE

OUR JEALOUS GOD
Love That Won't Let Me Go
BILL GOTHARD   ISBN 1-59052-225-7
(Available October 2003)

God's intense jealousy for you is your highest honor, an overflowing of sheer grace. And when you understand it better, it becomes a pathway to countless blessings.

THE POWER OF CRYING OUT
When Prayer Becomes Mighty
BILL GOTHARD   ISBN 1-59052-037-8

Bill Gothard explains how a crisis that is humanly impossible is an opportunity for God to show His power—the moment you cry out to Him.

THE FIRE THAT IGNITES
Living in the Power of the Holy Spirit
TONY EVANS   ISBN 1-59052-083-1

Tony Evans reveals how the Holy Spirit can ignite a fire in your life today, transforming you from a sleepwalker into a wide-awake witness for Him!

GOD IS UP TO SOMETHING GREAT
Turning Your Yesterdays into Better Tomorrows
TONY EVANS   ISBN 1-59052-038-6

Are you living with regrets? Discover the positives of your past. Tony Evans shows how God intends to use your experiences—good, bad, and ugly—to lead you toward His purpose for your life.

SMALL BOOKS
BIG CHANGE

www.bigchangemoments.com

BIG CHANGE

THE HEART OF A TENDER WARRIOR
Becoming a Man of Purpose
STU WEBER
ISBN 1-59052-039-4

SIMPLY JESUS
Experiencing the One Your Heart Longs For
JOSEPH M. STOWELL
ISBN 1-57673-856-6

SIX STEPS TO SPIRITUAL REVIVAL
God's Awesome Power in Your Life
PAT ROBERTSON
ISBN 1-59052-055-6

CERTAIN PEACE IN UNCERTAIN TIMES
Embracing Prayer in an Anxious Age
SHIRLEY DOBSON
ISBN 1-57673-937-6

THE CROSS CENTERED LIFE
Experiencing the Power of the Gospel
C. J. MAHANEY
ISBN 1-59052-045-9

THE DANGEROUS DUTY OF DELIGHT
The Glorified God and the Satisfied Soul
JOHN PIPER
ISBN 1-57673-883-3

RIGHT WITH GOD
Loving Instruction from the Father's Heart
RON MEHL
ISBN 1-59052-186-2

A PRAYER THAT MOVES HEAVEN
Comfort and Hope for Life's Most Difficult Moments
RON MEHL
ISBN 1-57673-885-X

THE LOTUS AND THE CROSS
Jesus Talks with Buddha
RAVI ZACHARIAS
ISBN 1-57673-854-X

SENSE AND SENSUALITY
Jesus Talks with Oscar Wilde
RAVI ZACHARIAS
ISBN 1-59052-014-9

SMALL BOOKS
BIG CHANGE

www.bigchangemoments.com